Surviving College with Bipolar Disorder

By Christina Marie

Everything in this book is true. Only names of people and places have been changed.

## Acknowledgements

I would like to express my deep appreciation to everyone who helped me with this book. I thank my mom for her support, editing, and generosity in making a cover for me.

I would also like to thank my main editors: my aunt, Laura Cooper and my great friend, Dora Kohnke. Their revisions helped me push myself to make this book more polished than I ever imagined. To the countless others who looked at my book before I finished it, thank you.

Thank you to Freepik.com for the Smiley faces and graduation cap designs.

# Table of Contents

Part 1 ...................................................................5

    Fall Semester Freshman Year.............................6

    Spring Semester Freshman Year ......................22

    Fall Semester Sophomore Year.........................25

    Spring Semester Sophomore Year ...................39

    Fall Gap Semester..............................................44

    River College.....................................................57

    Reflections.........................................................65

Part 2 .................................................................73

    What Works........................................................74

    What Doesn't Work ...........................................79

    What it Takes to Achieve your Dreams...........81

# Part 1
## My Story

# Ch1

## Fall Semester Freshman Year

The crisp September air marked new beginnings for me. There was a tinge of chaos in the wind as the seasons made their abrupt switch. As the weather changed so did my entire way of life. The start of college gave me a taste for how fun life could be. I joined the sailing team and immediately had a group of friends to hang out with. I was spending my time learning, sailing, and partying and I couldn't have been happier. For the first month of school, my life was at its peak, but it soon took a turn for the worse.

My excitement turned to elation as I started enjoying life a little too much. I could hardly contain my happiness and wanted to scream, yell, and laugh as loud as I could. As I walked to a sailing get-together, I told my dad on the phone that I loved college and I was high off life. I was ecstatic about what I was learning in class, hugely charismatic, and making lots of friends. My happiness was contagious and I found that people wanted to be around me and thought I was hilarious. Given no one had ever met me before; they all probably thought this was my real personality.

My emotions compelled me to dance around my room at every opportunity so that I could release my utter exuberance. I would walk around campus smiling from ear to ear, listening to music sped up four times its normal speed. I was wired all day and could not fall asleep at night.

My state of health slowly declined as the lack of sleep got to me. In class I stopped taking notes and would write in huge letters across my notebook—I WOULD RATHER BE SAILING. I was full of interesting thoughts; when I sat down to do homework, I found myself writing sticky notes of ideas that popped in my head instead of focusing; all my thoughts were life changing and had to be saved. My mind was running a mile a minute and kept me entertained at every second. My behavior was slowly becoming more and more obscure

I went away for a sailing regatta and was only able to sleep for a few hours before the race. Early in the morning, I decided to walk around the building and try to memorize what kind of cars were in the parking lot.

We had great wind at the regatta. My elated state combined with my enjoyment for sailing left me incredibly happy all day. I strategized to figure out the best side of the course and how the wind was shifting. My extreme energy let me hike out the whole time, determined to keep the boat flat so that we could maximize our speed.

When I got back to campus I walked around and noticed how looking at shiny, new things made me feel massively happy while looking at old, beat up things made me feel depressed. I thought I was making amazing discoveries about how the world worked. I wanted to share my findings with everyone so that we could fill the world with only things that kept us in a positive mood.

Soon, I began to alternate between understanding reality and being perplexed by it. One minute, I would be walking around campus thinking I was on breaking news across the country and laughing out loud; the next, I would berate myself for acting so weird.

As my health grew progressively worse, paranoia began to strike. At this heightened sense of awareness, fear became a much scarier and intensified feeling; I was afraid even to go to the bathroom. I began to think Google was stalking me by tracking all my activity on the internet, viewing me through my laptop camera, and even sending spies to watch me from afar.

I kept walking from my dorm to a new friend's house and back after coming back from the regatta. I would hang out with them and then leave abruptly, only to return later. During one of the visits I told the people there that I thought something was wrong with me but I didn't know what to do. One girl suggested that I go to Health and Counseling services and so I did.

I walked into the Health and Counseling services bawling my eyes out. I was an emotional wreck and believed that the staff members were secretly my family members even though the workers had no resemblances of them and I was hundreds of miles away from home. I filled out the initial appointment form with complete honesty while waiting in the lobby, my tears blurring the page as if attempting to deny the reality I had just written. Desperate for someone to help me, I jumped out of my seat when my name was finally called.

However, I hated the serious discussion I had with the therapist. My attention span was as short as ever and I was looking for someone to help me. But this appointment was doing just the opposite. I felt like the counselor was judging me, it seemed she had made up her mind that I was a very troubled young woman the minute I had walked in the door. Of course, she had read my form and learned about my excessive drinking and partying. Instead of asking me about what I had been up to recently, she focused on these two behaviors as being the root of my problems. After a horrendously long time of talking about why I had been resorting to these poor life choices, she ended the appointment and sent me on my way. But I was rapidly escalating towards the height of my hysteria and had no idea where to turn next.

Well, maybe there is nothing wrong with me. I should head back to my dorm and do some work for my Chemistry test tomorrow. Gah I got a C on the first one so I really have to do well on this one but I have barely studied for it.

Ok, now that I am alone in my room I think I should just listen to music and do some quick dancing around. Woooo hoooo. This is so fun!

Alright I really need to study now.

Molecular weight: the sum of the atomic weights of all the atoms in a molecule.

Wait what? I need to read that again.

Molecular weight: the sum of atomic weights of all the atoms in a molecule.

Molecular weight: the sum of atomic weights of all the atoms in a molecule.

Molecular weight: the sum of atomic weights of all the atoms in a molecule.

Okay I am not understanding this at all maybe I should just do some problems.

What is life?

Okay molar mass of the empirical form times x equals molar mass of the compound. So the molar mass of $CH_2O$ is 12.01 g + 2.02 g + 16.00 g.

What is religion? Why were my parents so religious and then suddenly not?

Okay now 30.03 g times x equals 120.12 g.

Maybe I was meant to be religious. Oh maybe since my parents both discovered religion in college I have to too.

Alright x = 4 so the answer is $(CH_2O)4$ or $C_4H_8O_4$.

I need to do some googling to figure this out right now.

Okay so my parents became devout Christians in college. Hmmm, what is this here? Born Again Christianity ... what's that? This website wants me to say this prayer out loud and it will let me start over my life with a blank slate. What the heck is this? They are prying on the weak and taking advantage of people! People are coming to these websites when they are in a time of crisis and so desperate for help they will try anything. Born Again Christianity is prying on people who are vulnerable and pulling them into this cult-like following. This is so messed up! Why did my parents fall for this? Waaaaa! Waaaaaahaaahaaa!

Oh my gosh. I cannot possibly study right now. I am getting so distracted.

Ahhh I'm so stressed out. Wait, I smell smoke. Hmm, it's kinda foggy in here. Oh my gosh, is the building on fire? Ugh, don't be ridiculous the building is not on fire, the fire alarm would be going off.

But maybe this building is actually Hell. Maybe I have tapped into a different reality where I can see the truth. Everyone else thinks they are in a college dorm but really this is a place where people who have sinned go.

Oh my gosh, the lights outside are moving towards me! I think I can actually feel the hairs on my neck standing up straight with fear. What is going on?

I need to listen to some upbeat music so I am not so frightened.

Ahhh. There, I feel happy again.

But wait, the names of the songs on my music player are ridiculous! Oh I know, the names are just figments of my imagination! Life isn't real, I am just dreaming it all up!

Ahhh this song is scary! Skip it, skip it fast!

Well I guess I still have to study for my test tomorrow.

There is no way I can get myself to study on my own.

I'm gonna text my crush, Charles, and see if he'll study with me.

Well what should I do before he texts back?

I'll just get all my stuff packed up and start heading towards his dorm.

Oh no he texted me back that he is too busy studying to help me. Well since I am already walking I'll just go to his dorm anyway.

Bring. Bring. Bring.

He didn't answer.

Waaaaa! Waaaaahaaahaaa!

No one can help me but I need so much help! What is wrong with me???

9.1.1.

"Brighton 911. What's your emergency?" the phone operator said.

Hi. There is something wrong with me but I don't know what it is. I feel incredibly emotional and am having weird thoughts. I need help.

"Where are you located?" he said.

"On Joseph College campus at the WWC dorm."

"Okay, you can stay on the phone with me until we get there."

After I called 911, I was transported to Jeffrey Hospital in an ambulance. The police officer waved a flashlight in my eyes to which I responded, "I am not taking drugs, why would I call 911 on myself if I was on drugs." Being in the ambulance was surreal for me. I completely forgot who I was. I asked the EMTs to please give me the worst room in the hospital because, "I have been cruel and need to be punished."

I was brought to a small room that was a little scary as it had a metal wall and loud vents. I stayed in that room for hours and hours as different nurses and doctors came and went. One doctor was particularly frightening as he showed no emotion and was completely serious when he talked to me. I assume this is something Psychiatrists do in order to evaluate their patients but it was one of the scariest conversations I have ever had.

Eventually, I was admitted into the Mental Health ward. I closed my eyes as I was wheeled to the ward with no clue what was going on. When I was put in my bed, I refused the medicine and demanded that a picture be taken of me.

That night I did not sleep. Instead, the cool air of the hospital frightened me. I thought I was in Hell. I thought it was strange that Hell was actually cold and lifeless, unlike the fiery dungeon I had imagined it to be. Once, when cold air blew through the room, I believed the devil himself had entered in an invisible state.

Over and over again, I held my breath as long as I could. I thought that I had to do this for the rest of my life and that for each breath I held, I would bring a baby to life on Earth. So this is what people in Hell do, I figured, their punishment is to help keep life going on Earth. That was one of the scariest nights of my life.

Every morning when I woke up, I would hope that I would no longer be in this odd and frightening place. I felt like the same day was playing on repeat, like in the movie Groundhog Day. It felt torturous. The nurses scared me in their uniforms, and I think they were afraid of me too. At one point I got out of bed to explore the ward and decided that I was in some sort of Purgatory and that I was Jesus. I found two glass doors next to each other, one dark: the entrance to Hell, and one lit up: the gateway to Heaven. I felt I had to choose one door to go through.

I wasn't wearing my contacts, but I was so out of touch with reality that I thought the blurred colors and shapes were an accurate portrayal of where I was. On the first night, I had taken my contacts out and now had a different nurse who didn't know I needed them. I went to a group without being able to see and just guessed at the answers to the crossword puzzle we were playing. The other patients laughed at me and I had no idea how everyone else was getting the questions right.

I ate a meal with the other patients and thought I was eating the Last Supper. Then I thought that I had switched lives with the girl sitting across from me and that I was now the opposite of everything I was before. I must have said something weird because my nurse then asked me if I was seeing things. Although I hadn't been, the question prompted me to try to see things in the smoke outside the window. I told her I could see dead people and was promptly taken back to my room. I remember crying, wondering what I had done wrong. Since I had been refusing the medicine, I had no idea where I was or what was going on.

When I watched TV I thought it was shouting out my name to get my attention, telling me to simply ask for help. It seemed the news anchors were laughing at me for not taking this simple step that would help me get better. It didn't help that the birth date on my wristband was one day off from my real birthday; I thought I had been given a new life where my birthday was slightly different.

When the weekend arrived, my parents visited me. I asked them if I should take the medicine. When they said yes, I finally agreed. I was able to sleep for the first time in days as soon as they arrived. My doctor told me I was going to be treated for bipolar disorder but that they were not able to make an absolute diagnosis yet. Finally I had an explanation for my odd behavior but I hung on the thread of hope that I might not have this intense disorder. When the medicine kicked in, I just about returned to my normal self immediately. The nurses were amazed at my transformation. I even told one what I had thought about the two doors, and we laughed about it together.

For the two weeks that I was unable to leave the hospital or use a computer, it was hard to keep up with my classes. So, when I finally got out of the hospital I was greeted with an overwhelming load of work to catch up on. Luckily, most of my teachers were understanding; my professor for my Coffee Ecology class even let me make up quizzes at home, trusting I would not cheat. I also found an incredibly helpful TA who sat down with me and taught me much of the chemistry that I had missed.

The list of challenges I was facing seemed endless. My manic episode occurred right around the time when freshmen began forming friend groups, so missing two weeks of classes left me a bit behind in meeting people. Not to mention, I had to deal with the fact that everyone I had met so far knew I had gone crazy and disappeared for two weeks. It was also hard at first to remember to take medicine every day. I would leave class early if I realized I had forgotten to take it. My roommate, who had previously been great friends with me, stopped talking to me when I got out of the hospital.

My living situation quickly became very uncomfortable and contributed to the depression I experienced later in that semester. Luckily, the upswing of my manic episode lasted for most of the rest of the semester, giving me enough energy to catch up in all my classes and still go to sailing practice some days.

As finals week approached, depression started to set in as it sometimes does following mania. I would burst into tears whenever I was alone and made sure to talk to my mom every day. When my roommate was in the room I would go to the deserted bathroom on the first floor of my building. Though it was rarely used, sometimes people would come in and see me crying. I would cry every time I sat down to study and had to push myself to be productive through my violent tears. I learned all types of techniques to cheer myself up and would reward myself with snacks and TV shows for studying for a certain amount of time. I found that forcing myself to study amidst crying uncontrollably worked. If I kept pushing myself, I would eventually get immersed in my work, holding off my tears for a little while.

I could hardly keep myself from crying in public but constantly pushed myself to go to class and to the library anyway. I became better at concealing my emotions, though fighting back tears so often gave me massive headaches. Even still, there were some things that were just too hard to stay emotionally neutral about. For my final paper in my writing class I wrote about my experience of going to the hospital. When I was asked to read my essay, I knew I would not be able to keep concealing my pressing desire to cry and broke down. I had never been so emotional before. During my depression the tears would come on suddenly and unexpectedly, often for no apparent reason and sometimes around a certain time of day.

Studying for finals when I was so depressed was the hardest things I had ever done, and getting through it gave me confidence that I could do anything I worked hard at. After the seemingly endless hours of studying for exams had finally paid off, I was incredibly relieved when the semester was over and I was able to go home for winter break.

# Ch 2

## Spring Semester Freshman Year

After winter break I was excited to go back to school; a month with my family was just what I had needed, and I was hopeful my depression would not return. But the harsh winter left me feeling cold and lonely, and I soon found myself crying every day again. Sailing had stopped for the winter, so all the free time I suddenly had left me feeling lost. I was incredibly miserable and hated the idea of continuing living the way I was, so I took a medical withdrawal for the semester. I was hoping to go abroad where I wanted to teach surfing lessons, but my mom insisted on me taking classes at Harkin Community College to keep on track to graduate in four years. So, I ended up doing just that.

I hated taking classes at Harkin Community College. Used to living in a nice town with a highly rated public school, going to school in a more dangerous, poverty filled area proved to be a shocking transition. Though I had never taken easier classes in my life, I was not getting all A's like I knew I should have been. I knew I was capable of more and was ashamed that I wasn't able to do my best work. My mom told me that she was really worried about me when I was home that semester.

She said I slept probably 20 hours a day when I could, and my doctors didn't seem to know what to do.

As I was struggling with my life, my brother was just beginning to turn his around with some new found motivation to stop playing video games all day and instead start working aggressively to lose weight. He pushed me to run with him and lose the weight I had gained from depression and being on Zyprexa. He ran slowly with me at first, and we increased both the distance and the speed at which we ran over the months. When I would slow down and want to give up, he would encourage me, pushing me to run even faster. The endorphins from exercising made me feel much better and helped me to move out of my depressive state. Running five miles a day gave me confidence that I could move forward with my life. I knew I did not want to waste away my days living at home and taking courses at a community college; I wanted to regain my independence and be proud of where I went to college.

When the summer came, I got a job working outside and spent every day at my grandparents' beach house where I had a great group of friends. Being busy and constantly surrounded by people who cared about me helped me to finally escape the long depression that had consumed me. By the end of the summer, I felt ready to take on my next year of college.

# Ch 3

## Fall Semester Sophomore Year

As my mom and I drove back to school I was excited and ready to move on with my life. We went to the welcome barbeque for the sailing team and I reconnected with old friends. We laughed about how I saved so much money by taking classes at a community college and joked about how I should do it again.

The sailing team still loved to drink and from what my parents told me, I would not have to worry about another episode for a long time, so I didn't change my lifestyle. I went back to loving the college life.

I found out that while I was on medical withdrawal, my spot as a Medical Technology major was filled. My advisor recommended I switch to majoring in a similar major with a public health concentration but I did not want to do this. The public health concentration wouldn't prepare me to take a board exam and to become certified to work in a clinical lab, like my previous major was designed to do. I was extremely driven to graduate as a Medical Technology major, so I figured I would work it out somehow.

A few weeks into the semester, the first round of exams came along. The stress from all of them hit me hard, so I made a quick appointment with my psychiatrist. Here I cried uncontrollably and told him how my mood had been fluctuating and I felt like I had extra energy at times and felt like crying at others. He told me to go to the emergency room and that if I didn't, someone would come looking for me.

I went to the ER and tried to explain why I was there, but the employee didn't seem to understand. At this point in my life I was too afraid to tell people I had bipolar disorder, so I was just telling them my symptoms. When I was finally called, the ER nurse treated me horribly, getting visibly frustrated with me because to her I seemed fine, like I was just wasting her time and didn't really need to be there. This treatment made me upset, and I began to cry relentlessly. When I finally saw a doctor, she said there was not much she could do because she had not been monitoring my medication and did not want to make any changes. I got a note from the ER to give to my professors so I could have more time before my tests.

I left the ER angry at the lack of help I had gotten there. I wasn't feeling well, similar to how I had felt the year before, and I was afraid I was only going to get worse. My frustration was through the roof and I decided to get blackout drunk to spite the hospital since I believed they did a very poor job of treating me. I felt helpless to the impending doom of an episode that I knew was starting. I thought I had done the right thing by going to see my doctor and spending half my day in the ER but I didn't get the help I needed and I felt so frustrated that it seemed I was going to get worse whether I kept trying to stay well or not. At the moment I left the hospital I thought to myself, "Fuck it", I just tried so hard to get the help I needed and it didn't work. I awoke the next morning to find myself alone on a couch in a house I had never been in before. My jacket, wallet and room key were nowhere to be found, and my parents were coming that day for parents' weekend. I especially needed to find my room key so I could pull myself together quickly and hide what a mess I was from my parents. Luckily, my phone was just about the only thing I still had with me, and my alarm had woken me up in time to go to sailing practice later and meet up with my parents.

When I met up with my parents, we went to a crepe restaurant for lunch. I conversed very loudly and quickly; perhaps a trained psychiatrist would have suspected something, but to my parents I just seemed enthusiastic to see them.

Since I partied so hard on Friday, I stayed in Saturday night to try to catch up on sleep in hopes that I would be able to avoid going back to the hospital. The extra sleep that night wasn't enough to keep me sane, and my thoughts began to spiral out of control.

That Monday night, I began feverishly reading on the Internet, taking in massive amounts of information about exorcism and other odd topics. As I laid in bed unable to go to sleep, I thought my heartbeat was getting weaker and felt I was close to death because of how hard I partied on Friday. The ceiling tiles in my dorm room appeared to be moving, which terrified me. All night I was deeply afraid of the dark and unable to sleep. As the morning slowly approached, I left my room to watch the sunrise, thankful that it would finally be light out again.

Sitting in bed that morning I heard an ambulance go by and thought it was a figment of my imagination. I took it as a sign that I was God and the world was dying because I hadn't saved it yet. Determined, I started writing up a plan to save the world. I tried to incorporate everything I had ever learned in school and be systematic about it, but I looked at the plan later and thought it seemed extremely odd. Well aware that I was not feeling healthy, I went to my Microbiology professor and asked for more time for a quiz that I missed that morning, telling him that I woke up thinking I was God and that I had to work on a way to save the world instead of going to class. He responded that he didn't know anything about waking up and feeling like God, but I would have to take the quiz in a few hours because he was planning on grading them soon.

I can't believe my professor is making me take this quiz today! How the heck am I going to memorize my enormous stack of flashcards? Fuck it, I'm just going to head over to the library, get serious and do this.

Ah, I am so emotional right now. I need to resist my urge to cry. I'll just try to be as emotionless as possible. There, that blank stare is doing the trick.

K I'm in the library, I'll find a new spot.

Biofilm: an aggregation of microorganisms sticking together on a surface

Parasite: an organism that benefits while a host is damaged

Gram positive: dark blue, thick peptidoglycan

Gram negative: pink, thin peptidoglycan

I really need to appreciate the little things more in life. I never just sit and admire how nice the sky is.

Ok here it goes.

Biofilm.

Ugh I forget.

Parasite.

Can't remember that one either.

Gram positive.

Nope.

Gram negative.

Nope.

Hmm I wonder what the music I like says about my character? Are the songs that I like messages to me?

Ok I'll read through them all again and then test myself.

Ahhhhhhhh. I still can't remember them.

That was a funny conversation I had with Trish this morning about how you shouldn't try to over analyze life because it will drive you crazy.

Well I'll go through my flashcards 20 more times and hopefully I will start remembering them.

Still can't remember anything. But the thoughts I keep having are so interesting, I absolutely need to google them. I think googling them is what I was meant to do in this moment of time and it is all part of the larger plan of my life.

Alright I'll just set up my computer, put on some music, and start searching.

Why is the world so black and white?

Hmm, not finding anything interesting. I'll have to keep digging.

Here, this is what I was meant to find.

This is that test that most people have taken in their lives! I remember this being on the door of my elementary school class room. We tried to read the words spelling out colors but the ink they were printed in was a different color. It was so hard. Well this website is telling me that when you take this test it is really finding out if you are inherently good or evil. If you are inherently good you can read the green words. If you are inherently bad you can read the red words. So those teachers are just finding out who is inherently good or bad! Wow that is so messed up that people are inherently good or bad. That means this world is so messed up. How do we solve crime if the people committing the crimes are inherently bad? They will never be able to be changed.

Oh my gosh. Looking out the window, the world looks so much clearer when my eyes are filled with tears. Maybe I need to die for the world to be a better place. Maybe I have to sacrifice myself like Jesus.

Ahh, the girl sitting down next to me is an angel. She has the most blonde hair and blue eyes. I know she's an angel. She is coming to me help me because she knows I need it.

Ok, I'll just close my eyes and hold my breath over and over again until I die. This angel sitting next to me will help me through it.

One-one thousand. Two-one thousand. Three-one thousand. Four-one thousand. Five-one thousand …

Ok, thirty-two seconds. I'll do more next time.

*Daydream, Daaaay dream. I fell asleep
beneath the flowers. For a couple of hours. On a
beautiful day. Daydream. Daaaay dream. I dream
of you amid the flowers. For a couple of hours.
Such a beautiful day.*

Wow. This song is a message to me that life
is a dream. We are all just dreaming!

One-one thousand. Two-one thousand.
Three-one thousand. Four-one thousand. Five-one
thousand ...

One-one thousand. Two-one thousand.
Three-one thousand. Four-one thousand. Five-one
thousand ...

This is so sad that God is going to sacrifice
me. I love life so much. I am going to miss all my
friends so much.

Oh, my friends are here in the library
cheering me on! There is a whole gathering of them
around me, everyone I have ever been friends with
is here. They all understand how hard it is for me to
go through this.

One-one thousand. Two-one thousand.
Three-one thousand. Four-one thousand. Five-one
thousand ...

Why haven't I died yet? I think I need to try harder and actually make choking noises.

One-one thousand. Two-one thousand. Three-one thousand. Four-one thousand. Five-one thousand …

This is weird, my body is starting to shake. Okay a white light is beginning to shine down on me. I think I'm about to be lifted out of my chair and taken.

Tap tap.

"Ahh!" I open my eyes after having them closed for 40 minutes.

"What are you doing?" says the EMT.

"I'm trying to kill myself by holding my breath."

"You know that isn't possible right?" he says.

"Yeah but what if I did it? I would prove that the nature of reality is not what we think it is. The world is so messed up"

A new EMT swoops in, "Hi, I'm an EMT. Do you have any prior medical conditions?"

"Yeah I have bipolar disorder"

"Okay we're going to take you to Jeffrey hospital, can you get in this stretcher?" She asks.

"Can't I just walk out."

"No, you have to get in the stretcher." She insists.

"Fine."

After being transported, I once again sat in a small room for hours before I was admitted. My coach came to visit me and was astounded by how long I had been sitting in one little room with only a hospital bed for.

The whole time that I was meeting with doctors and nurses, I pretended that I was fine and did not have bipolar disorder. I seemed to be doing a great job of convincing them at first, but said some weird things to my mom on the phone when I thought I was alone. Since the hospital had someone monitoring me, that person must have relayed the message.

Finally, I met with the final doctor who was going to admit me. He said to me, "You have bipolar disorder", and I broke down into tears. I had been desperately trying to believe that I was fine and having someone tell me that I had this disorder was incredibly discouraging. I could no longer hang onto the thread of hope that I was normal. The official diagnosis had been made. It felt unbearably unfair that all the pain I'd suffered in my college life was due to an inherited condition, yet I had to accept this as my truth. I was overwhelmed by the seemingly impossible challenge of learning how to manage my moods and prevent future episodes. I felt like I had done everything in my power to avoid going back to the hospital this year and yet it still happened. I contacted a doctor right when I felt like I was unwell and made a trip to emergency room to no avail. I knew I needed help that day and the medical community did nothing for me. I guess the truth was that by the time I noticed my manic symptoms, it was already too late.

As my doctor entered my information into the computer, he revealed I was being admitted on the same day as the year before. We were both surprised by this unusual coincidence.

The hospital I was admitted to that day was the same one I had been to the year before. It was fairly modern, and I felt safe and comfortable there. They updated some of their rules, so this year I was allowed to use my laptop in my room, making my stay immensely more tolerable. I was better able to keep up with my school work. I kept to myself, focusing on staying up-to-date with my studying and didn't go to many of the groups offered for patients.

I felt that going to the groups the year before had made me feel more disabled. I felt like the groups did not do much to help us be ambitious about the future and were more about complaining about why our lives were so hard. I decided I would rather think about working towards making my life better.

I had a lot of friends visit me in the hospital. It meant so much to me that I had so many people in my life who supported me during tough times instead of judging me for struggling with my mental health.

This time in the hospital, I took the medicine right away and didn't act out at all. I had gained weight, so I was switched from Zyprexa to Seroquel. I thought that one positive of being hospitalized was that it was an opportunity to easily change the medications I was taking since I wasn't totally happy with them. I finished up my second fall semester at Joseph College without getting too depressed.

# Ch 4

## Spring Semester Sophomore Year

When I returned to school in the spring, I started getting serious about getting better. My doctor advised me to stop drinking, so I did. A friend that I had texted lots of crazy things to during my freshman year episode high-fived me at a party for not drinking. I took it as her way of forgiving me for being weird to her. I was relieved and felt like I was finally getting some control of my life back.

I went to therapy regularly although I always ended up crying at the appointments, leaving me upset and unable to study afterwards. I hated seeing a therapist; it felt like a testament that I could not live my life on my own. The constant reminder every week that I had to see someone to talk about my problems kept me perpetually thinking about the bad things in my life. I was always thinking about what I should say at my next appointment to avoid awkward silences. I also felt like therapy was putting some blame for my disordered life on my own thought patterns and experiences. I really felt that when I was healthy I had perfectly normal thought patterns and that I did not have a traumatic experience to cause my first episode. I knew my disorder was genetic because my dad had bipolar disorder. To me, the best way to manage my disorder would be to learn how to recognize when I was getting a little manic much earlier so that I could contact a doctor about changing my medication. Having two episodes on the exact same day two years in a row, I felt their causes could have something to do with the season change and that I might not be able to prevent myself from starting to feel manic in the future but rather would have to learn how to act when the exhilaration started creeping in.

But for now I felt far from ecstatic, I was slowly growing more and more depressed as the semester went on. It was hard to have fun with my friends because they all would get super drunk at parties on the weekends. Feeling like I had tried avoiding alcohol and that it clearly wasn't working, I decided I should start drinking again so that I could have more fun in my life. However, my steady decline in happiness continued. I would cry every time I walked home from class and whenever I was in my room alone. Again, I started talking to my mom on the phone a lot.

About half way through the semester, I decided that my depression was getting so bad that I just wanted to run away from my seemingly horrible life. I tried not drinking and I was incredibly depressed during that time. Then I tried drinking thinking I would be happier on the weekends but of course that didn't work either. Again I felt like I was trying everything to get better but nothing was working. I was extremely depressed and the medication did not seem to be preventing it. My grades were suffering from my deep depression so I decided the best course of action would be to take a medical withdrawal from school. Luckily, my mom had bought an insurance plan that allowed me to withdraw late in the semester (since I was hospitalized for an extreme medical emergency) and still get a full refund.

At my doctor's appointment the day I admitted that I wanted to withdraw, it was hard to say my plan out loud because I felt like such a failure admitting it. In attempt to make withdrawing seem more like my doctor's advice instead of my own idea, I tried to lead the conversation in the right direction so that he would ask me if I wanted to take a medical withdrawal. Apparently, I didn't succeed because he wasn't saying anything along those lines. I eventually said it and broke down into tears.

For my last night out I got really drunk with two friends. The day before, my friend had suggested that I write an email to the team saying I was withdrawing, so everyone at the party knew I was leaving. I don't think people really understood why I was leaving, because I did an excellent job concealing my depression and forcing myself to attend classes and go out on weekends. It's just that every moment I had alone I would violently cry. I guess it finally hit me that my life was not headed in the direction I wanted. I had no intention in trying to come back to Joseph College. As far as I was concerned, I needed big changes in my life.

On the day I left school I texted my best friend, Trish, to come over and say goodbye. My room was far too messy to hang out in, so we sat in the common room next door. She brought chocolate, and she told me something along the lines of, "Don't forget, you're awesome" when we parted ways.

Back at home, I enrolled in an outpatient program at a hospital nearby. There were different lessons for us each day and a time for us to talk to each other and counselors about our problems. This treatment was unlike anything I had received before and it was really helpful. We were encouraged to figure out how to improve our lives for the future. An important thing I learned there was to not feed my emotions, but instead catch myself before it got out of hand. Crying often made me think of other sad things which only made me cry even more. I learned that if I gave into this behavior I would feed the emotion until it was too big and powerful to handle. I realized that it was important to monitor my mood and detect when my emotions were starting to get too strong. Instead of letting my thoughts get the best of me when I was crying, I learned to do something to cheer myself up and that this was easier to do before the sadness became too powerful.

I waited out the depression and spent my days after the hospital program sleeping excessively. I got a job as a sailing instructor and looked forward to spending every day outside in the summer.

I seemed to be failing in so many aspects of my life and I felt incredibly discouraged. However, I had relentless drive to slowly pick myself up and get on track.

# Ch 5

## Fall Gap Semester

My mom thought it would be best for me to live at home and take classes nearby for the rest of college. This was just about the last thing I wanted. I came back early from my grandparent's beach house that summer to practice with the tennis team at Barton State University. Unfortunately, when it came time to register for classes, I realized I was unable to get into the science courses I needed in order to stay on track to be a Medical Technology major. I decided to take Anatomy and Physiology II, Microbiology, and General Biology at Franklin Community College.

I avidly searched the Internet for colleges with a Medical Technology program. After going through the list of schools in the northeast countless times, a new school suddenly jumped out at me. River College was medium sized, private and seemed like the perfect fit. I confirmed my assessment when I visited and totally loved it. It was the only school I applied to, and I needed to get in for the spring semester or it would take me longer than 5 years to complete college. I had pretty average grades in college so far. Luckily, I had much better grades in high school and good SAT scores for the school I was applying to. I worked hard in the classes I was taking and went around to all my professors half way through the semester so I could supplement my application with my current grades. I had all A's. Soon, I heard back that I was accepted to the college of my dreams.

So far, everything was going well but I wasn't completely done making mistakes yet. I went to visit my old school and fell back into my old lifestyle. A week or two later, I was experiencing my third manic episode in three years.

I was not doing well and needed to go to the hospital, and my mom suspected that. However, when she said something about it to me, I didn't respond well. I yelled at her, saying there was nothing wrong with me, that I knew how to manage my emotions perfectly. Despite my claims to my mom, I was not fine.

I know I need to study, so I'll try my best to hold off the tears. Okay I studied long enough to take a break. I'll doodle on this paper here. Hmm, why am I thinking about my manager at the restaurant I work at right now? I know, she is trying to telepathically contact me. I'll try to figure out what she is asking me.

"Christina, why are you so sad?" she asks.

"I don't know I feel like I must have had a terrible childhood to make me feel this way."

"That's silly, she said. "Maybe you are upset about something right now... what are you upset about?"

"I'm mad that my parents don't know I'm crying right now."

Gosh that was weird I just had a conversation with someone else in my head. Was that real? Did I make it all up?

I need to call my friend. "Hey Trisch, whats up? I feel like I understand how the universe works. Today I figured out that police motorcycles play a soundtrack of a human heartbeat at a frequency that only dogs or really sensitive people can hear. It is a tactic they use to control us."

"Oh really?" she says.

"Yeah I think the president is evil. Okay, bye!"

Alright I need to color-code this chart so I can understand everything. Let me run to CVS.

Wait, is the car behind me following me? I need to lose them. I'll accelerate around this turn so they can't see me anymore and take a quick left turn before they catch up.

Phew, I lost them. I can continue to CVS now.

Alright got my colored pencils. Now let me pay for these.

"Your total is 2.44" says the cashier.

Hmm, I forget my pin, I'll guess at it. Oops I must have guessed wrong.

"Haha, I forgot my pin, I'll just put it through as credit"

"Oh haha, I always do that. Here you can slide your card again," the cashier says.

"Thanks," I say. "Wow how could I have forgotten it?"

"Haha, I have those days too. Have a great rest of your night." The cashier gives a little wave.

"You too!" I say, feeling energized from the fun interaction. I should be talkative with cashiers more often.

Alright, I've got my colored pencils. Now I'll color all the gram negative organisms grey and the gram positive ones green. Okay, all the citrate positive organisms can have some blue. All the indole positive organisms can have some purple. Wow, this is the smartest way I could have studied. I am so smart!

Okay, time to go to bed even though I don't feel tired.

I've been lying here an hour and am still wide-awake. I should use my phone a bit. What should I do? Oh I know; I'll concentrate on all the people in my phone's contacts one at a time. For each person, I will envision their DNA becoming stronger so that they won't have any more illnesses.

Well I can't sleep so I guess I should just entertain myself with my thoughts.

Woohoo, it's light out! I can wake up! Wow I have so much energy even though I didn't sleep. I'm gonna go downstairs and check my computer. Hmm, maybe I'll go on facebook. Oh, I need to help change the world so I will post some stuff. Okay, I just realized everything is backwards right now. I need to convince the world that people do and say things that they don't want to all the time.

Okay, done. I have to go to class and take my final now.

Wow, everyone parked so perfectly. I must be in some alternate universe where everyone parks perfectly and no one makes any mistakes.

Hmm, they are installing security cameras? I ask the friendly construction worker, "They want to watch our every move?"

"Haha, yup" says the construction worker.

Maybe if I concentrate really hard I will be able to pick up on other peoples' thoughts as they are taking this test. Hmm, not working. Wow, I keep having to reread the question over and over again in order to understand it. Oh look, I'm the last one in the room.

"You almost done?" asks my professor.

"Yup."

That was such a fake smile she is probably actually impatient with me. I'm never the last one finished with a test. This is weird.

Phew, I'm done.

A friend in the hallway asks, "Want some chocolate?"

"Sure, I love chocolate."

Why am I hanging outside of this room? I'm gonna leave now.

"See you guys!"

Hmm, my cell phone says SOS whenever I am in my house (I have terrible cell phone service in my house). That must mean that my house is dangerous. I should stay away from it.

I had a job at the time that required me to go around making purchases at various stores to test credit cards. So, I was in my car on the way to a store when I got distracted. I had my iPod plugged in and thought the songs playing were the ones I was thinking about; I thought I was controlling my iPod with my mind. I saw school buses driving around and called my brother in tears, afraid that kids were being taken away in masses somewhere. My brother told me he thought I needed to go to the hospital, but I still truly did not believe it. I thought my GPS was routing me to an unknown destination. I started driving around aimlessly. I decided I needed to go to the North Pole and spread the spirit of Christmas to everyone because I believed people these days had lost the spirit of Christmas. I was quickly using up all my gas, but I thought if I didn't believe my gas would run out, it wouldn't. I felt like I had transcended into a new universe where everything looked the same, but life was just better.

I stopped in a grocery store just because and tried to figure out what to buy. I thought that there were things in the store that I was meant to buy and that I had to find them. I walked around and stopped at the Hallmark section. I spent a long time trying to find the perfect Christmas cards to give to my family. Next I walked around until I stumbled upon Tide-to-Go pens which I decided to buy. A few minutes later, I decided that I shouldn't spend money and left the store without anything.

I got back onto the highway and eventually found myself in a tunnel.

This tunnel is so scary. The city is so scary. What if there is a terrorist attack? I need to stop before I get any further. I'll do a U-turn to turn around. Whoops... I guess I didn't think this through; I can't drive the opposite direction as the traffic. I'll just park my car facing the wrong way in the fast lane and get out. I should blast Christmas music, since Christmas is approaching. That way, everyone will get in the Christmas spirit as they drive by.

Which way should I go? I'll keep going the same direction I was driving. Wait no, I'm going the wrong way. I should go the other way. How do I figure out the right path in life? I guess I have to stay away from the extremes and stay in the middle. So which way do I go?

Oh no, I think this way is starting to angle down. What if this tunnel is leading me to Hell? Oh look, someone is rolling his window down, I'll go talk to him.

"What are you doing?"

"I don't know which way to go!"

"I think you should go back to your car."

He seems really nice but he doesn't understand, I'm gonna keep walking.

Oh look a police man. Oh he's trying to catch me. This'll be fun I should try to run past him. Giggling, I try to run past. Oh he caught me. He's pushing me against his car. What do I do so that he doesn't arrest me? I'll tell him I love him. Yes, that'll work. I yell, "I love you! I love you! Why are you doing this to me? I love you!"

Once I was in the police station I refused to tell them if I had a medical condition or what medicine I was taking, although I did reveal I was taking the element "Li" in the table of elements. I guess they didn't know what that was. I did not want them to know I was bipolar because I thought I could convince them to release me. I told them that I thought the camera they took my picture with was scary. I was trying excessively hard to keep my mood upbeat because the police station was frightening to me, and the feeling of having scary thoughts when manic is so horrible. Eventually, they transported me to Granby Hospital where I spent the next week and a half. Luckily I was not arrested; their only charge was to temporarily suspend my license.

For the most part, the hospital was nice, but their psychiatric ward was really run down. There was an old security system with cameras and televisions that weren't in use anymore. The hallways and railings in the hallways looked like they hadn't been cleaned in years and the showers in our rooms didn't even work. Unfortunately, no one warned me about the showers, so I took a shower and flooded my room. I realized the drain wasn't working, but I really did not want to end my shower before I rinsed out my conditioner, so I didn't. The oldest doctor saw this as a sign that I was "Fuzzy". I found that term to be extremely insulting.

After my mishap, the staff directed me to the communal shower, and it was by far the grossest shower I had ever seen. I don't think I've ever been more disgusted by a shower, not even when camping. The tiles were yellowed and there was dirt and grime all on the floor. There were chairs crowding the shower room as well. The only shower head was handheld, making it impossible to apply soap, shampoo, or conditioner while also having the water running.

A young resident was in charge of my case and I thought she did a great job. When I told her that I had trouble focusing on school work while on my current medication, she switched me to a different one. She said it would target a different area of my brain and might not interfere with my ability to focus. While I was in the hospital, I would read books to try to gauge whether I could focus on the medication or not.

I was released earlier than they thought I should be because they wanted me to be able to celebrate Christmas with my family. Instead of tapering me off of the antipsychotic in the hospital, I would have appointments after being released so that my dosage could be slowly lowered. I wanted to stay on a low dose of the medication because I thought I needed an antipsychotic to help prevent future hospitalizations. I spent the next month recovering and kept my plans to transfer schools, despite my doctor's suggestions to wait longer.

During the time I spent at home that winter, I started reading self-help books and tried every strategy I could to turn my life around. I started envisioning my changed life every night and thought about what I wanted my life to be like in the future.

I wanted to succeed in school. My whole life I had been dedicated to my studies and I wanted to get back to this. I also wanted to major in Medical Technology because I wanted to prove to myself that I could graduate with a difficult college major. I also wanted to make better friends who cared about school like myself.

# Ch 6

## River College

When I got to River College, it took a little while for me to find friends that fit the new lifestyle I wanted to have. I went to a party and we decided to play baseball, a heavy drinking game. The next morning I was so disappointed in myself for going back to my partying behavior. I realized that I would have to stay away from people who drank heavily in order to avoid it myself and I never drank like that again.

I contacted the captain of the ultimate frisbee team to find out if I could join. Anyone could go to the intramurals so I decided I would try it out. I dragged some of my friends along with me and I had a lot of fun. I was amazed by how nice everyone on the ultimate team was. After a few weeks they invited me to a party and to my excitement, they didn't drink a lot.

The new friends I made at frisbee helped to build my confidence and turn my life around. I started planning my studying ahead of time so that I would not get stressed out. This was working well for me, and my grades were way up from what they had been at my old school. Every day I would reflect on my behaviors and decide if I was acting a little manic or depressed so that I could take early action and prevent these feelings from getting worse. I found a doctor that I liked and who was not afraid to prescribe me a safe antidepressant if I really needed it. Most importantly, I never gave up on my dreams, even when my life was falling apart and it felt like I could never succeed.

While I was getting much better grades and feeling better about my life, it was hard to escape my seemingly cyclic manic episodes. At the end of my spring semester, I was staying up late playing ultimate frisbee because our only gym time to practice was from 11 pm – 1 am. Around finals week, I grew really stressed out because my Methods of Medical Technology course was so difficult. I had actually started crying in class earlier that day when my professor went over the material for the final practical. Fortunately, sneaky as I am, no one noticed. I felt really emotional and not right when the practical time came and had to work really hard to suppress my tears while I was taking it.

I called my mom and my boyfriend to tell them that I didn't feel well and I was worried I would have to go to the hospital. On the phone with my boyfriend, Ralph, I was energetic and told him I felt like I was dreaming. I did some more homework on campus before walking back at night.

I felt especially scared walking back to my dorm and realized that I was feeling a little paranoid.

I felt that I would be in really bad shape the next day if I didn't get enough sleep, so I called Ralph and told him I wanted to go to the hospital. He suggested I tell my two friends that I lived with so that they could drive me. It was extremely hard to go to my friends for help because they didn't know I had bipolar disorder, and I was afraid of what they would think of me. It also made me feel like a failure and that I could not keep my life together to stay out of mental health hospitals. I wished that I could just stay healthy. I mustered up the courage to ask Janice and Cindy to take me to the hospital and let Ralph talk to them on the phone. They didn't ask many questions and drove me right to Gartland Hospital. They stayed with me while I went through the long admission process to keep me company. When a doctor came and asked me questions, I let them stay in the room with me. This was the first time I had let friends in on my secret struggles with bipolar disorder and it was a relief to have others start to understand my condition.

Later that night, Ralph arrived after his two hour drive. He held my hand and reassured me that the psychiatric ward wouldn't be that bad. In the morning when I woke up to him sleeping in a chair, hunched over a desk, my volatile emotions surged through my body, begging me to cry; it was then that I realized how much he cared about me. Ralph, Janice, Cindy and some other friends visited me throughout my stay at Gartland Hospital as testament that the friends I had made so far at River College in my efforts to turn my life around were kindhearted and irreplaceable. My parents visited me on the weekend and my mom didn't want to tell any of my family I was in the hospital, but I told her it would be nice if she did.

Gartland Hospital was the grossest one I had been to yet. The rooms smelled like pee and were very visibly dirty. The unit was outdated and there was a scary knob on the wall to turn on medical gas. The staff was incredibly busy and treated the patients horribly. I had to wait three hours for my school work after it was delivered. Getting anything done was far too much of a chore to bother since the staff was so busy. Just to ask a nurse a simple question I would have to wait ten minutes. While most of the other hospitals I had been in had many visiting hours, this one only had one hour a day. A staff member washed some of my clothes for me when they were dropped off, but apparently put them in a mislabeled bag afterwards, so they were lost for about a week. My doctor did not tell me much about how he was treating me and did not give me a chance to ask any questions. On the day I was admitted, I noticed he drastically lowered my mood stabilizer dose overnight, and I had terrible mood swings in the hospital. I went to a nurse, crying because my mood stabilizer was lowered so drastically, but she was not sympathetic at all.

I had asked my friends to drive me to the hospital so I thought I would be a voluntary admit and be able to leave when I wanted but instead I got marked down as involuntary. Although I was not manic when I was admitted to the hospital, I still was kept there for a week and a half. That might not seem like a big deal but being trapped in one run-down building filled with employees who don't care about their patients was terrible. Although my parents assured me I would be released eventually, I really felt like I might be kept there forever.

Thankfully, I was able to study for my upcoming exams while in the hospital. I would have made Dean's list that semester, but I had to take a temporary incomplete for one class and took the final at the beginning of my next semester. All in all, my hospital stay this time was less discouraging because I knew it was precautionary.

The next year was my first without a manic episode. It felt like such a break-through and turning point in my life. I wish I could've celebrated it but no one seemed to take note of it. Instead of letting my mania develop without noticing, I told my doctor when I started to feel more energetic and he was able to increase my antipsychotic. Going without a manic episode and feeling really healthy gave me confidence that I could stay out of the hospital if I continued to manage my sleep, lifestyle, and medication. I'd had so many times in my college career where I seriously doubted my ability to graduate, and this was the first time I could actually envision myself finishing college.

My senior year was filled with accomplishment and wonderful memories. I made it though all my difficult Medial Technology courses with great grades. I managed my time and stayed on top of my work so that I never got stressed out about tests. After a long study session I would text my best friend Caitlyn, "If I come home right now will you have tea with me?" and she would respond, "Of course!". I had so much fun living in my house with close friends. We would set up pranks on each other, play keep-away in the kitchen, make funny videos, and have epic exercising adventures.

The friends I made at my new school were a huge help to me turning my life around. Unlike my old friends, they made studying their first priority. My friends and I would usually go to a party one night of the weekend and on the other night hang out in the house baking cookies or watching a movie. I was also able to talk to them about my disorder and they did not judge me. They provided me with much needed emotional support as well. My great new friends made my life a hundred times more manageable and enjoyable. I learned how finding the right crowd can make a huge difference in enjoying life.

The week leading up to graduation I marveled at how far I'd come since my freshman year at college. I changed from getting blackout drunk every time I went out and being completely helpless when it came to knowing anything about monitoring my mood to being able to drink very little or not at all, constantly monitor my moods and sleep, get good grades, and have super fun friends. Transferring schools allowed me to start over fresh and find friends who were better influences. I turned my life completely around and I was honestly a little amazed by it. I thought back at how I was able to avoid having a manic episode my senior year by paying keen attention to my behaviors and working closely with my doctor and it gave me hope that I had broken the cycle and would be able to keep maintaining my healthy state as long as I worked hard at it.

My energy on graduation day was one of exhilaration to walk across the stage, optimism for the road that led ahead, and pride for having accomplished a great challenge. Everyone was cheery and the weather could not have been better. The sun kissing all of our faces, glimmering across the river, and enriching the colors of nature made my field of vision seem as though I was looking through a high definition lens. When I received my diploma I felt like I had just succeeded in not letting even the greatest of hardships stop me from getting what I wanted.

# Ch 7

## Reflections

In my grade school years I was shy, incredibly obedient, rarely cried, and as I got older, afraid to drink alcohol. But I started to change at the end of high school. Suddenly, I started doing worse in school, got emotional when people talked about sad things, and would crave danger. I would drive 60 mph on small, windy roads with speed limits of 35 mph just for the rush it gave me. Without a doubt, bipolar disorder changed my personality. I took four years of battling the illness before I could find the best medications, figure out how to control myself and return to who I originally was.

Looking back, I am amazed that I had such odd thoughts during my manic episodes and could not recognize that they were not normal. Once I am healthy, I am embarrassed by how I acted during my mania. I have found that an important part of getting healthy was to be able to see obscure thoughts from mania an incongruent with my current reality and to stop believing in them.

I am so thankful for how well the medicine worked. Its effectiveness proved to me that I really do need to take it, and I still rely on it to keep me sane today. I can't tell you how many people—friends, TAs, coaches—told me not to take the medicine I was prescribed. At first, I struggled with the idea of taking a medicine that would change my personality. Despite my doubts, it is now five years later and I am really healthy.

I found that going to a smaller school where the professors got to know and trust me, I was able to get extensions for exams much more easily. At the larger school I went to, I had a professor lose the accommodation sheet I gave him at the beginning of the semester and not grant me extra time because he didn't remember me.

I've always been very independent and have tried to avoid relying on others as much as possible: I much preferred to figure things out for myself. So, as you can imagine, asking for help in order to manage my illness has been one of the hardest things for me to do. I hated asking teachers to postpone exams for a later date. Having to rely on my teachers for help left me feeling helpless and stripped of the independence that I once prided myself on. After just asking for an extension, I would go home and cry on and off for the rest of the day. For me, using accommodations was not the best solution since it left me so upset. Instead I worked extra hard so that by the end of college I wouldn't need them anymore.

Although this book may portray me as a person who is seriously and obviously ill, most of the time I act normally, and no one would ever suspect I had bipolar disorder. For me, mania usually slowly builds up, but the serious symptoms and weird thoughts usually only last a few days before they land me in the hospital. Depression lasts longer, but I have done a good job of masking it from other people.

When I tell people I have bipolar disorder, I usually get responses such as, "Wow, I would never expect that" or "You do a good job of hiding it." I hope sharing this can help reduce the stigma towards people with mental illness and help the public to learn that people with mental illnesses are only sick when their illness isn't under control.

I think if we educated students about mental disorders then our culture would become much more accepting. Also, having others understand could help prevent tragedies. If my Microbiology professor had understood bipolar disorder maybe he could have called 911 and got me into a hospital before my symptoms got worse. I think there is such a huge stigma against mental illnesses because people don't understand them.

Through my experiences and those of my dad, who also has bipolar disorder, I believe the health care needs to improve a lot. Getting well with bipolar disorder needs to really come from within, but health care can certainly help us along. I have seen my dad in and out of mental hospitals for three months straight, and I think it is a testament to the system not being perfect.

Educating patients and setting up a real plan for getting healthy once leaving the hospital would greatly improve the health care system. I learned a lot of useful information when I went to an outpatient program, and I think this needs to also be incorporated into inpatient programs. To further increase chances of success, it would be nice if each patient could have appointments to meet with the same doctors they had during their hospitalization to make sure they are following through with the plan they made to get healthy.

Bipolar disorder is such a serious disease that I am surprised I was never handed a book to teach me how to handle my life. Patients with bipolar disorder should be given a text book and worksheets to teach them how to: detect when their mood is becoming slightly manic or depressed, know what to do to avoid becoming more manic or depressed, learn how to cooperate with their doctor, make friends that will be supportive, change to a healthy lifestyle, and the list goes on. I know that these resources exist but I think that doctors need to play a more active role in recommending them to their patients. Reading one novel about bipolar disorder is not enough; I think patients should be treating this like they would treat doing school work.

In my experiences with bipolar disorder, I had four manic episodes in four years. Starting after my first manic episode I was seeing a psychiatrist and taking my medication as prescribed the whole time. I really think my doctors should have taught me more about how to avoid becoming manic again. Doctors should teach their patients what kind of behavior to look out for so that individuals can detect mood changes even earlier. I also believe that patients should be able to contact a doctor at any given moment. Waiting a few days for a doctor to respond to a call about feeling slightly manic is unacceptable. If it is not possible to have a doctor available at all times then patients should be given instructions for what to do if they detect a mood change. I know this is the case for some doctor's offices but I think it should be more universal. Concrete plans should be made to allow patients to avoid getting sick again.

There is also room for improvement inside the mental health hospitals themselves. One needs to be extremely regimented in order to turn one's life around, so I think it makes sense to start this in the hospital. In order to build a structured life while still in the hospital, patients should be encouraged to exercise every morning, whether their workout consists of walking on a treadmill or running, and go to groups every day. These groups should be much more educational and demanding than the groups I have come across and should be focused on improving one's life. I also think the staff should be much more caring towards the patients. In my experience, there are some hospitals that need radical change where the staff members are hardly compassionate.

I also think the whole medical community is not educated well enough about mental disorders. I have heard from people working at hospitals that there is gossip about the patients that need multiple security guards and are taking mood stabilizers. Employees say things like, "Why didn't he go somewhere else". This shows that the employees do not understand that mental illnesses make individuals act out in ways they never would when their illnesses are not under control.

In my own life, I hope to help make my ideas for improving mental health care to come to fruition. I see mental health patients as normal people who just need to work a little harder to overcome some difficulties in their lives. A disorder like bipolar can really make a person act out of character, so it is important to recognize that this behavior is due to the disease.

In this book I give a lot of examples where I went against doctors' advice. This is not to say that I think doctors have bad advice. My experiences where I have been under the care of a psychiatrist but still have had an episode despite taking my medicine as prescribed have taught me that I can't put all my faith in my doctors. I know they have my best interests in mind but I think I know best what I need to do to stay healthy and lead a successful life. I have come to learn what I need to do in order to stay healthy and successful. I am good about calling my doctors way ahead of time when I think I need a change in medicine. I know it worked well for me to not go to therapy while I was in college but this will not be true for everyone. I didn't listen to doctors when they told me to take a break from school because I knew that going to school was something that I really wanted to do and not going would leave me very dissatisfied.

I hope sharing my experiences will not only spread awareness about bipolar disorder and how it can affect a person, but also give the hope and advice necessary to help struggling bipolar students succeed and be a story that can help those suffering feel less alone. According to the National Institute of Mental Health, the prevalence of severe bipolar disorder is 2.2%. This is a lot higher than I would ever have guessed because very few people talk about having bipolar disorder.

I understand that bipolar disorder can seem scary and dangerous to someone that does not have it. When I found out my dad had bipolar disorder it very much scared me so I know that the disorder can be difficult to understand. It was not until I was diagnosed with bipolar disorder myself that I understood it. I feel so normal when my symptoms are managed so I know that when bipolar disorder is under control the individuals who suffer from it are no different from anyone else.

# Part 2
## My Advice to You

# Ch 1

## What Works

In order to get good grades in college with bipolar disorder you have to get serious and mature fast. Most importantly, you should establish a bedtime and get a healthy amount of sleep each night. For me, only sleeping a few hours a night is a huge red flag that I could soon go into psychosis. In addition to monitoring sleep, you should keep drinking under control or not drink at all and avoid drugs. Heavy drinking will affect your moods and alcohol often interferes with medication. Using recreational drugs can trigger psychosis. You should also be sure to take your medicine as directed and find medicine that works for you. Following these three steps can transform your chaotic, episode dictated life into one that is controlled and symptom free.

It is difficult to make these three steps to health a priority in college. Students often sacrifice sleep for studying and partying, and it is often easy to get caught up in binge drinking and drug using, as both are prominent on most college campuses. If you are stuck with friends who encourage any of these behaviors, it is a good idea to make new friends. You could do this simply by joining different clubs or if this is too hard it might be easiest to transfer colleges for a fresh start where you can seek out others who don't drink or keep drinking to a minimum, care about their studies, and have healthy sleep schedules.

It might seem like finding friends who follow these three guidelines for being healthy will be impossible, especially if your current friends are far from following them. I thought this too, but then I took a semester off and thought hard about how I should change my life and the kind of people I wanted to surround myself with when I transferred colleges. I ended up becoming great friends with two girls who didn't drink, but were still fun and sociable. They were just what I needed; I could go to parties with them, have a great time sober and leave at a reasonable hour together so that I could get enough sleep. Even though finding people who do not drink is rare at many colleges, it is possible and with determination you can do it. If you have trouble finding friends who don't drink, you can also seek out sober housing at schools or chose a school rated for high levels of sobriety.

If you are stuck in an unhealthy lifestyle and would like to change, an important step to take is to have a vision for what your successful life will be like. Just like professional athletes envision perfect pitches before they go on the mound, you can envision a perfect lifestyle. Before I transferred schools each night I would visualize myself drinking at a much slower pace than usual. When I got to my new school I found that I really would drink more slowly. Seeing myself drink slowly over and over again helped me to change my habit in my everyday life. You can do this with any habit you want to change or any lifestyle you want to start experiencing. I also read countless books about how to improve my life.

An important part of being healthy is surrounding yourself with positive influences. As habit, humans like to conform to fit in with groups. This means you will conform and start acting more like the friends you have. You must choose friends with values and lifestyles that match how you want to spend your own life.

As you learn about bipolar disorder and your moods, you should also learn your triggers and what calms you down. Learning these are preventative steps so that you can better handle mood swings. So, pay attention to the types of situations that lead to mood swings or episodes. For me, all my episodes have occurred around the time of a big exam, so I know that stress over schoolwork is a big trigger for me. This means I plan my studying far ahead of time so that I do not get in a situation where I waited until the last second and do not have enough time to learn everything I need to for a test. I also know that if I am having a bad mood swing I can calm myself down by drinking a glass of water, calling my mom or boyfriend, or listening to music. Knowing what to do during a mood swing ahead of time allows you to act promptly when one attacks.

It is important to analyze your behavior and decide if you think you are acting normally. Signs of mania are irritability, decreased need for sleep, taking risks you normally wouldn't, and (sometimes) weird thoughts. If you detect any of these early warning signs you should contact your doctor to adjust medication levels and tell close friends and family to watch after you and to convince you that you need to go to the hospital if your symptoms get worse.

Another tip I have is to find a doctor you like. Your doctor is going to have a big impact on your health and you are going to see him or her regularly. So, it is important to find someone that you not only like, but also trust to manage your medications correctly. My doctor gave me his cell phone number so he is available for me whenever I have a moment of distress. I have called him about being stressed out about tests, and he has given me great advice.

Additionally, be sure to convey how you feel to your doctor. Your doctor is not going to know that you need a medication change if you don't tell him or her your symptoms.

For the first few years that I had bipolar disorder I was never prescribed an antidepressant and I had to endure horrible deep depressions. After having six doctors who never suggested an antidepressant, my seventh doctor did and it helped alleviate my sadness immensely. Of course, not everyone reacts to medications the same so you should be sure to discuss this with your doctor. Antidepressants can trigger mania so they are not always a good choice.

Perhaps the most important element of care for bipolar disorder is taking medications. It is important to be extremely dedicated to taking meds and know that your health relies on you taking them. Even when you feel 100%, know that you must still take your medications. I find it easy to trust in my meds maintaining my health because of how they instantly brought me back to reality when I was experiencing my first episode and was first treated for bipolar disorder. After taking my first few doses of medication, I snapped back to reality, leaving behind my belief that the hospital I was in was some kind of purgatory. The medication enabled me to understand exactly where I was and what was going on with me.

My last piece of advice is to never give up on your dreams and know that you are still capable of achieving everything that you desire. There will be times when it seems like your life is falling apart and you can never succeed. It's these times when it is most important to persevere and know that once you get through them, start improving and stay dedicated to remaining healthy, you will be able to reach your goals. Not only will you be able to reach your past goals but you may also find that surviving such a life challenge has made you stronger than ever and has left you with even bigger aspirations.

# Ch 2

## What Doesn't Work

Now that I've told you all I have learned about staying healthy with bipolar disorder I will tell you about why I was unsuccessful at staying healthy at the first college I went to. While my daily routine at the time was much like that of a typical college student, I had many bad habits. After my first episode, I didn't think I would have another one for a long time. I was mistaken.

First of all, I violated the three basic steps of staying healthy with bipolar disorder. Instead of getting the necessary amount of sleep before a test, I often pounded energy drinks so I could stay up all night cramming. I partied, drank a lot, and would sometimes forget if I had taken my medication or not.

I didn't realize my lifestyle was so bad for me because all my friends lived lives like me. This reiterates my point about surrounding yourself with values and lifestyles that you want to have yourself. My friends would binge drink and pull all-nighters to get schoolwork done. But my friends weren't the only ones behaving like this; I went to a party school and this kind of behavior was easier to come by than not.

Another reason I was unsuccessful was that I overbooked my time. I was on a club sailing team with the demands and time commitment of a varsity sport without any of the accommodations that a varsity athlete would get. I would wake up early and take multiple classes in a row so that I could get to practice each day. By the time practice was over I would eat dinner and be exhausted. I would have to take a nap in order to stay awake while doing homework, thus interfering with my sleep schedule.

Looking back, it's hard for me to believe that I didn't realize how unhealthy and overbooked my lifestyle was and how it was not conducive to me staying out of the hospital. At this point, hadn't yet made any changes to my lifestyle after my first episode, and so I found myself back in the hospital a year later.

# Ch 3

## What it Takes to Achieve your Dreams

As I mentioned earlier, the first step to achieving your dreams is to have a vision. You should think about your vision every day and before you go to sleep, to convince yourself that it is achievable.

Next you must believe in yourself and disregard people who doubt you. Even when counselors and doctors ask me if I want to take time off from school, I often didn't. This allowed me to finish college in five years. Stay ambitious and keep pushing through your workload. If needed, take some time off but be sure to still take a class or two.

It is important to develop relentless drive and ambition. With every set back, you must come back stronger and not let yourself get beat up. I analogize it with sports: if someone steals the ball from you, you can't get down on yourself, you have to come back at them with more intensity and get the ball back. Never doubt your ability to achieve your dreams, even when the going gets hard.

A strategy that may help you achieve your dreams is planning. Planning allows you to take one step at a time so that you are not overwhelmed. For example, long-term goals such as graduating college may seem daunting, while more short-term goals such as taking a few classes or getting through one semester seem achievable.

If you want to achieve all your dreams with bipolar disorder you also have to accept this: you will have to work harder than others to keep your life in order. You will have to develop discipline to go to bed at the right time every night, organization and planning in order to avoid stress, and self-restraint to not drink too much (or at all) or use drugs.

In light of accepting you have to work harder than others, it is also important to find the advantages of bipolar disorder and not focus on the negatives. Bipolar disorder helps me to be more creative and unique than others and it gives me motivation and drive to strive towards huge personal goals. My experiences with psychosis have allowed me to see the world completely differently than most are able to.